Surviving 9-5 Rat Race

Armie Bright

Published by Armie Bright, 2024.

SURVIVING 9-5 RAT RACE

First edition. March 11, 2024.

Copyright © 2024 Armie Bright.

ISBN: 979-8224617692

Written by Armie Bright.

Table of Contents

SURVIVING
9-5 RAT RACE

Strategies for Success, Resilience, and Financial Wellness

ARMIE BRIGHT

PART 1 WHAT ARE YOU MADE FOR?

CHAPTER 1: Stuck in the Matrix

So, you've found yourself trapped in the daily grind of a desk job, feeling like a cog in the corporate machine. Maybe you're even starting to resent it, feeling like you're stuck in the Matrix, punching in and out day after day with no real sense of purpose or fulfillment. But hey, guess what? You're not alone, and you're not doomed to spend the rest of your days chained to your cubicle. That's why you picked up this book, right? To uncover the secrets to breaking free from the monotony and reclaiming control of your life. Well, buckle up, because we're about to embark on a journey of discovery together, and trust me, the truth is more liberating than you could ever imagine.

Trust me, deciding to stick with a desk job over diving into the wild world of entrepreneurship might seem like the safe bet, but let me tell you, there's a lot more to it than just playing it safe. It's like choosing the well-paved path over bushwhacking through the entrepreneurial jungle—sure, there might be some exciting discoveries out there, but sometimes you just want a smooth ride.

Think about it: when you punch in and out of your desk job, it's like clockwork. You know exactly when your workday starts and ends, giving you the freedom to plan your downtime without worrying about business debts or looming crises. It's like having a work-life balance built right into your schedule, allowing you to leave your work at the office and fully enjoy your evenings and weekends.

Plus, let's talk about simplicity. With a desk job, you've got your tasks laid out for you, plain and simple. No need to juggle a dozen hats or manage a team of employees—just focus on what you do best and get it done. It's like having a clear path forward, free from the distractions and uncertainties that come with running your own business.

And don't even get me started on the perks of not being on call 24/7. Sure, being your own boss might sound glamorous, but who wants to be tied to their phone at all hours of the day? With a desk job, you can clock out at the end of the day and truly disconnect, knowing that your work will be waiting for you when you punch back in.

So yeah, maybe being a business owner has its thrills and spills, but there's something to be said for the simplicity and stability of a desk job. It's like cruising down the highway in a reliable sedan—sure, it might not turn heads like a flashy sports car, but it'll get you where you need to go without breaking a sweat. And sometimes, that's all you really need.

1. Navigating the Path of Predictability

In the realm of the 9-to-5 grind, predictability often gets a bad rap, but let's consider the flip side: predictability can actually be a comfort. Knowing what to expect day in and day out provides a sense of stability and routine that many find reassuring. After all, there's something to be said for the familiarity of a predictable job—the same tasks, the same coworkers, the same office banter. It's like slipping into a well-worn pair of shoes; comfortable, reliable, and easy to navigate.

But here's the thing about predictability: it extends beyond just the job itself. In many companies, you'll find that the people and attitudes are remarkably similar across the board. Sure, the faces might change, but the underlying culture remains consistent. There's a certain comfort in knowing that, no matter where you go, you'll encounter familiar personalities and dynamics.

Now, let's talk about WFO—Working From Office—versus WFO—Working From Outside. While the allure of remote work is undeniable, there's something to be said for the structure and boundaries that come with being physically present in an office. Picture this: a literal wall between your work life and your personal life. When you're at the office, you're in work mode—focused, productive, and ready to tackle the day's challenges. But when you step outside those walls, you're free to leave work behind and immerse yourself in your personal life without the constant pull of emails and deadlines.

And speaking of walls, let's talk about building walls—metaphorical ones, that is. When you have enough savings tucked away, you're not just building a financial barrier against uncertainty; you're also erecting a wall of confidence and self-assurance. With a healthy nest egg to fall back on, you can hold your head high and command the respect you deserve. People notice when you're financially secure, and that sense of stability commands respect in both your personal and professional relationships.

And once you've earned that respect, something magical happens: you gain the power to say no. No to unreasonable demands, no to toxic relationships, no to anything that doesn't align with your values and priorities. It's a liberating feeling—the ability to set boundaries and prioritize your own well-being without fear of repercussion.

So, in the end, while the 9-to-5 grind may seem mundane on the surface, there's a certain comfort and security to be found within its predictability. And when you combine that with the power of financial stability and self-assurance, you unlock a world of possibilities—a world where you can build walls, command respect, and say no with confidence and grace..

1.2 Work-Life Balance

Ah, the delicate dance of work-life balance—it's like trying to juggle flaming torches while riding a unicycle. But fear not, my friend! Setting boundaries is your secret weapon in this epic quest for harmony. When the clock strikes "freedom" at the end of your workday, make it a grand ritual to switch off completely. Picture this: ceremoniously powering down your work phone and embracing the sweet, sweet silence of personal time.

Speaking of phones, here's a pro tip: keep 'em separated like a bouncer at a VIP club. Invest in separate devices for work and play, giving you the power to disconnect from professional demands when it's time to unwind. And hey, resist that sneaky urge to respond to work messages after hours—your time is precious, my friend, and it deserves to be honored.

Now, let's talk about handling those curious colleagues who just can't seem to grasp the concept of "off the clock." A friendly yet firm response is your golden ticket. Simply mention that you're off on a personal adventure or catching up on beauty sleep. And here's a sneaky little trick: tweak your commute address ever so slightly, adding a scenic detour to your journey. Suddenly, you're the elusive unicorn of emergency meetings, giving yourself the gift of guilt-free personal time.

And here's the cherry on top: prioritizing your well-being isn't selfish—it's essential for your sanity and happiness! By setting and respecting these boundaries, you're not just carving out space for yourself, but also cultivating a healthier, more fulfilling relationship with both work and play. So go forth, my boundary-setting warrior, and conquer the quest for work-life balance like the hero you were born to be!.

1. Employee Benefits

Let's talk about the goodies that come with punching the clock and clocking out feeling like a winner. First up, we've got the holy grail of benefits: healthcare coverage. Think medical, dental, and vision insurance all wrapped up in a neat little package. It's like having a superhero cape, except it's for your health! No more fretting over doctor bills or avoiding the dentist like the plague—these benefits have got you covered, literally.

But wait, there's more! Cue the retirement plans, aka your golden ticket to financial freedom. With options like 401(k) or pension plans, you're not just saving for a rainy day; you're building a cozy nest egg for your future self. And here's the cherry on top: employer contributions and matching programs. It's like getting a high-five from your boss every time you put money into your retirement fund. Talk about motivation!

Now, let's talk about everyone's favorite subject: paid time off. Say hello to vacation days, sick leave, and holidays—all with a paycheck attached. It's like hitting the pause button on work without hitting pause on your bank account. Time off isn't just a luxury; it's a necessity for recharging those batteries and keeping that work-life balance in check.

But wait, there's more! Strap in for some professional development opportunities. We're talking workshops, training programs, and even tuition reimbursement for those eager to level up their skills. It's like investing in yourself, with your employer cheering you on every step of the way.

So, as we navigate the ins and outs of the 9-5 grind, let's not forget the bigger picture. Let's dream of a life filled with rich experiences, debt-free and supported by a steady stream of passive income from savvy investments. With each benefit we embrace and every moment we claim for ourselves, we're inching closer to that life of abundance and fulfillment we've always dreamed of. Let's make it happen!

CHAPTER 2: Breaks and Boundaries

In the daily rhythm of a 9-to-5 job, there are ways to add a touch of spontaneity and ease without missing a beat. Let's start with lunch breaks—instead of rushing through, why not savor every bite? Whether it's trying a new spot or simply taking a stroll, make it a mini adventure to break up the day.

But why stop there? Look for little opportunities to take breaks throughout the day. Whether it's grabbing a coffee or stepping outside for some fresh air, these small moments of respite can make a big difference in how you feel.

Now, if you're someone who finishes tasks ahead of schedule, that's great! Just make sure to stay connected via your work phone, so you're still reachable if needed. It's all about finding that balance between efficiency and availability.

When it comes to mingling with coworkers, it's all about finding the right balance. While it's great to be friendly, it's also important to keep some boundaries. Not everyone in the office is your best friend, so it's okay to keep some things private.

And speaking of privacy, remember to keep your personal life just that—personal. Share bits and pieces, sure, but there's no need to spill everything. After all, a little mystery can make things more interesting, right? So, embrace the rhythms of the office, but don't forget to add your own little flourishes along the way.

2.1 Scheduled Break Times

Alright, let's jazz up the routine and make taking breaks a breeze! First up, let's talk structure. Establishing a routine with set break times is like building a cozy nest for your productivity to thrive. Think mid-morning pick-me-ups, mid-afternoon recharge sessions, and a designated lunch break to refuel. With a consistent schedule in place, you'll breeze through your day with ease, knowing exactly when it's time to hit pause and rejuvenate.

Now, let's get strategic with those breaks. Tune into your natural energy rhythms and workload flow. Schedule your breaks for those moments when your focus starts to fade—like mid-morning when that initial burst of energy wears off, and mid-afternoon when the yawns start to creep in. By syncing your breaks with your body's natural rhythms, you'll hit the refresh button at just the right moments.

But wait, there's more! It's not just about timing; it's about finding the perfect balance. Short, frequent breaks are great for maintaining focus, but don't forget to carve out longer chunks of downtime, especially during lunch. Use that time to kick back, recharge, and indulge in activities that nourish your mind and body.

Now, here's the cherry on top: communication is key. Let your colleagues and bosses know about your break schedule so they're not left wondering where you've disappeared to. This helps manage expectations and ensures uninterrupted me-time. And hey, if you're prone to getting lost in the hustle, set up friendly reminders to nudge you when it's break time. Your brain—and your productivity—will thank you later!

2.2 Hydration and Nutrition

Let's kickstart your journey to better health and productivity with a few simple steps that'll have you feeling like a superstar in no time! First up, hydration—it's the MVP of staying sharp and focused throughout the day. Grab yourself a trusty reusable water bottle and keep it within arm's reach at your desk. Make a game of it—see how many times you can refill it and aim to drink up regularly. Pro tip: setting a cute little reminder on your phone can be a total game-changer!

But hey, hydration isn't just about chugging water like it's going out of style. Load up on hydrating foods too, like juicy fruits and crisp veggies. Not only do they taste delicious, but they also give you that extra hydration boost while keeping your snack game strong.

Now, let's talk grub. Planning ahead is where it's at! Whip up some nutritious snacks and meals to bring to work, so you're armed and ready when hunger comes knocking. Think balanced meals with a little bit of everything—lean protein, whole grains, healthy fats, and a rainbow of fruits and veggies. Say "buh-bye" to those vending machine regrets and fast food blues—your body will thank you for it!

And hey, don't forget to take those well-deserved breaks! Step away from your desk, find a cozy spot, and really savor your snacks and sips. It's not just about refueling your body; it's about giving your mind a chance to chill out too. Bonus points for inviting your work buds along for the ride—bonding over snacks is always a win in our book!

So, there you have it—hydration, nutrition, and a sprinkle of socializing to keep you feeling fresh and fabulous all day long. Here's to healthy habits and happy vibes!.

2.3 Define Work Hours

Let's kickstart your workday with some game-changing tips to set you up for success! First off, it's all about setting those boundaries, my friend. Grab a pen and paper (or hey, use your smartphone if that's your jam) and jot down clear start and end times for your workday. Make sure to factor in any special requests from your boss or team. Once you've got those hours locked in, spread the word! Let your colleagues, bosses, and clients know when you're ready to rock and roll and when you're off the clock.

Now, here's where the magic happens. When you're nailing down your work hours, think about what makes you tick. Are you a morning person who's ready to tackle the world before sunrise? Or maybe you're more of a night owl who hits their stride after sunset. Whatever floats your boat, schedule your work hours during those peak times when your brain is firing on all cylinders. And hey, let's keep it real—don't bite off more than you can chew. Set realistic boundaries around your availability to avoid burning the candle at both ends.

Once you've got your groove going, stick to it like glue! Resist the urge to sneak in some extra work outside of your designated hours (unless it's absolutely urgent, of course). And hey, spread the word! Let your team know that you're off-duty during those precious off-hours, unless it's a dire emergency.

Now, let's talk tech. Embrace those handy-dandy tools to keep your work-life balance in check. Set up email autoresponders to let folks know when you'll be back in action, and don't forget to block off some personal time on your calendar. Your sanity will thank you later!

Last but not least, keep it flexible, my friend. Life's all about rolling with the punches, right? So, be ready to tweak your schedule when duty calls. Just make sure to keep the lines of communication open with your team and bosses. After all, balance is the name of the game. So, go ahead, rock those work hours like a boss, and remember—work hard, play hard, and keep that smile shining bright!

2.4 Communication Guidelines

Alright, let's dive into the world of communication guidelines at your 9-to-5 gig! Imagine it like laying down some ground rules for when and how to chat it up, both during and after the usual office hours. First off, let's pick our favorite ways to chat—emails for the official stuff, and quick instant messages for those speedy updates. Once we've got that sorted, it's time to spread the word to the team so everyone's on the same page and we can all zip through our to-dos without any hiccups.

Now, let's talk timing! It's super important to let everyone know when you're available to hit them back. Setting clear expectations about when you'll be around to chat can help ease the pressure to always be on call, giving you some breathing room to enjoy your off-hours.

And hey, emergencies happen, right? That's why it's handy to have a game plan for when things get urgent outside of the regular grind. Setting up some ground rules for what's considered urgent and how to handle those moments can keep everyone on the same wavelength when the unexpected pops up.

Tech to the rescue! Tools like email autoresponders and status updates on messaging apps can be lifesavers when it comes to keeping everyone in the loop about your availability. They're like your trusty sidekicks, making sure folks know when you're off-duty and how to reach you in a pinch.

Lead by example, my friend! Show your team how it's done by respecting their downtime and not bombarding them with messages when they're off the clock. By practicing what you preach, you're setting the stage for a workplace where everyone's personal time is valued and honored.

And remember, communication guidelines aren't set in stone! Keep 'em flexible and tweak 'em as needed based on how things are flowing. Your team's feedback is gold, so be sure to check in regularly to see what's working and what could use a little tweak. With clear guidelines in place, you'll be fostering a workplace where everyone feels respected and supported, leading to a healthier work-life balance all around.

2.5 Prioritize Personal Time

Think of it like the VIP pass to your own happiness and well-being—it's not just a luxury, it's an absolute necessity. So, why not treat yourself to some quality "me" time?

To make personal time a priority, it's all about setting boundaries. Picture this: you're the captain of your own ship, steering clear of work waters during designated personal time. Set those work hours in stone and let your colleagues know when you're off-duty. Trust me, they'll understand—and if they don't, a gentle reminder might just do the trick.

Now, onto the fun part: self-care! Whether it's breaking a sweat, indulging in a hobby, or simply chilling with your favorite people, make sure to pencil in activities that light up your soul. Block off that calendar like it's your own personal playground, because guess what? It is!

Here's the golden rule: learn to say no. Repeat after me: "Nope, not today!" Don't let extra work sneak its way into your precious personal time. Instead, focus on activities that speak to your heart and recharge your batteries. Remember, you're the boss of your time, and your well-being comes first.

And last but not least, keep tabs on how you're spending your personal time. Balance is key, so make sure to sprinkle in activities that energize you and leave you feeling like a superstar. Listen to your gut, follow your bliss, and remember that personal time isn't just a break—it's a vital ingredient for living your best life.

2.6 Say No When Necessary

In the fast-paced environment of a 9-6 job, learning to say no when necessary is essential for maintaining your productivity, sanity, and overall well-being. It's not about being rude or uncooperative; instead, it's about setting clear boundaries and prioritizing your time and energy effectively. Start by understanding your own capacity and workload. Recognize that taking on too much can lead to burnout and compromise the quality of your work. By being honest with yourself about what you can realistically handle, you empower yourself to make informed decisions about which tasks to take on and which to decline.

When faced with a request that you cannot accommodate, it's important to communicate your decision assertively yet tactfully. Express gratitude for the opportunity and explain your reasons for declining the request. Whether it's conflicting priorities, time constraints, or simply needing to preserve your energy for essential tasks, be transparent about your limitations. Offering alternative solutions or compromises can also demonstrate your willingness to collaborate and find solutions without overcommitting yourself.

Furthermore, remember that saying no is not a reflection of your worth or competence. It's a strategic decision to protect your time and focus on tasks that align with your goals and responsibilities. Practice self-advocacy and assertiveness in your communication, using confident body language and a firm tone of voice to convey your message effectively. By setting boundaries proactively and communicating your availability and workload clearly with colleagues and supervisors, you can minimize the need to say no and create a healthier work environment for yourself and those around you

2.7 Utilize Technology

Picture this: you're in the midst of your 9-to-6 grind, juggling tasks left and right like a pro. But hey, who said you have to do it all manually? Let's talk tech—the ultimate sidekick in your quest for workplace domination.

First up, we've got the heavy hitters: project management platforms like Asana and Trello. These bad boys are like personal assistants on steroids, helping you organize tasks, track deadlines, and keep the whole team in sync. No more messy email threads or frantic phone calls—just smooth sailing towards project success.

But wait, there's more! Say hello to your new best friends: Slack and Microsoft Teams. These communication champs make collaboration a breeze, letting you chat, video call, and share files with ease. With them on your side, you'll wonder how you ever survived the pre-digital era.

And let's not forget about the cloud—the ultimate game-changer in remote work. With Google Drive and Dropbox, your files are always at your fingertips, no matter where you are. So go ahead, work from the beach or your favorite coffee shop—your files will be right there waiting for you.

Now, let's talk about automation—the secret weapon of productivity ninjas everywhere. Email filters, scheduling tools like Calendly, you name it—these babies take care of the boring stuff so you can focus on what really matters. Think of them as your own personal army of efficiency.

But hey, the tech train doesn't stop there. Stay on top of the latest trends and tools in your industry, and you'll be one step ahead of the game. Attend webinars, workshops, and conferences, soak up that knowledge like a sponge, and watch your productivity soar to new heights.

So there you have it—your ticket to workplace nirvana, courtesy of the wonderful world of technology. Embrace it, wield it like a pro, and watch as your 9-to-6 hustle transforms into a well-oiled machine of success and satisfaction. All aboard the tech train—it's time to ride into the future!.

CHAPTER 3: Tackle problems

Picture this: You're stuck in a job that feels like a never-ending maze, each day throwing new obstacles and frustrations your way. Sound familiar? That suffocating feeling of being trapped in a stress-induced whirlwind can really take its toll, leaving you feeling drained and disillusioned.

Navigating this stress-fueled chaos might seem like an uphill battle, leaving you feeling like you're running on empty. The pressure to perform, coupled with the fear of falling short, can weigh heavily on your shoulders, sapping your energy and drive.

In the midst of this exhausting grind, it's easy to start questioning whether it's all worth it. The idea of breaking free from the suffocating grip of stress becomes more tempting by the day, whispering promises of relief and liberation.

But hold on a second—amidst the chaos and despair, there's a glimmer of hope. A tiny spark of resilience that refuses to be snuffed out. You're not alone in this struggle, and there are ways to reclaim control over your well-being.

5.1. Evaluate Options

Ah, the rollercoaster of decision-making! It's like being on a wild ride of emotions, right? From the thrill of anticipation to the nail-biting apprehension, it's all part of the journey. So, buckle up and get ready to navigate through the twists and turns of finding the perfect solution.

First things first, let's take a chill pill and step back to assess our options. Think of it like laying out a buffet of solutions—each one with its own tempting delights and potential pitfalls. Consider things like how feasible they are, whether they'll break the bank, and how much bang they'll bring for your buck. It's like playing detective, searching for clues to unravel the mystery of the perfect solution.

But hey, don't be surprised if you start feeling a tad overwhelmed. It's totally normal to have a mini freak-out moment when you're juggling all these factors. Take a deep breath and remind yourself that it's all part of the process.

Now, here's the kicker: there's no one-size-fits-all answer. Yup, you heard that right! Sometimes, the best solution isn't crystal clear, and that's okay. Instead of chasing after a mythical "perfect" choice, focus on picking the option that feels like the best fit for you and your goals. It's like finding the right puzzle piece to complete the picture.

And hey, if you find yourself stuck in decision limbo, you're not alone. We've all been there! Use it as a chance to flex those critical thinking muscles and dive deeper into the analysis. Don't hesitate to rope in some backup from colleagues or mentors for a fresh perspective.

5.2. Decide

When you're at the crossroads of decision-making, it's like standing at a buffet with endless options—exciting, yet a tad overwhelming! But fear not, my friend, for there's a method to the madness. Take a breather, grab a mental notepad, and let's break it down.

First off, gather all the deets. Yep, we're talking facts, figures, and maybe a sprinkle of intuition. Then, channel your inner Sherlock Holmes and sleuth out the potential outcomes of each option. Think of it as a mental tug-of-war, weighing the pros and cons, and considering how each choice might play out in the grand scheme of things.

Now, here's where it gets juicy. Decision-making isn't always as clear-cut as choosing between vanilla and chocolate (although, let's be real, that's a tough one too). Sometimes, you're navigating through a fog of uncertainty, juggling conflicting priorities like a circus performer on a unicycle. That's when you call in the reinforcements—trusted pals or wise mentors who can shed some light on the situation.

But wait, there's more! Making a decision isn't just about crunching numbers or consulting the Magic 8-Ball. It's about summoning your inner superhero, embracing that courage, and trusting your gut. After all, life's an adventure, and sometimes you gotta take a leap of faith, superhero cape fluttering in the wind.

5.3. Implement the Solution

As you dive into putting your solution into action, it's totally normal to have a few butterflies fluttering in your stomach. Doubt and uncertainty might try to sneak in, but trust in the process that brought you here. Remember, problem-solving is like a dance—it's all about taking steps forward, even if you stumble now and then.

Communication is your secret weapon during this phase. Keeping everyone in the loop—your team, your colleagues, even the big bosses—helps create a vibe of transparency and teamwork. Whether it's sharing updates, brainstorming ideas, or addressing concerns, keeping those lines of communication open is key.

Now, brace yourself—curveballs might come your way. But hey, that's where the real fun begins! Stay nimble, stay sharp, and be ready to pivot if needed. Challenges are just opportunities in disguise, waiting for you to flex those problem-solving muscles and come out stronger on the other side.

As you start to see your plan take shape, don't let up on the gas pedal. Stay laser-focused on that end goal and keep your finger on the pulse. Celebrate those small wins along the way, but remember, the journey isn't over yet. Keep that momentum going, stay proactive, and watch as your hard work blossoms into success.

5.4. Monitor Progress

Hey there, progress tracker! Let's talk about keeping tabs on how well your brilliant solution is doing. One nifty trick is to set up regular check-in points where you can gather your squad—key stakeholders or team members—for a powwow. These meetings aren't just about giving updates; they're your chance to soak in feedback, tackle any pesky issues head-on, and brainstorm fresh ideas. Think of it as creating a safe space where everyone's voice matters and magic can happen. But hey, it's totally normal to feel a bit jittery about sharing your progress, especially if you're still figuring things out.

Now, onto the fun part—data! Yep, we're talking numbers, surveys, feedback forms—the whole shebang. Crunching those digits helps you see the big picture and figure out if your solution is hitting the bullseye. Sure, it can feel like all eyes are on you, wondering if your efforts will pay off. But fear not! If you're feeling the heat, don't hesitate to lean on your squad for some backup and advice. You're not alone in this journey.

And here's the secret sauce: stay flexible like a yoga master! Things might not always go according to plan, and that's okay. Problem-solving is like a dance—sometimes you gotta improvise those moves. So if you hit a roadblock or your first attempt doesn't quite stick the landing, don't sweat it. Take a breather, dust yourself off, and get back in the game. Remember, every setback is just a chance to level up and come back stronger. You've got this!.

5.5. Adapt as Needed

As you dive into monitoring progress, brace yourself for unexpected twists and turns along the way. Yep, sometimes things don't go according to plan, and that's where the real fun begins! It's all about finding that sweet spot between practical problem-solving and acknowledging the rollercoaster of emotions that come with it.

Now, here's the secret sauce: feedback. Don't just listen to your own thoughts—open up those ears and gather insights from all corners. Your colleagues, stakeholders, and even data analytics have something valuable to say. It's like putting together a puzzle; each piece adds to the bigger picture, helping you fine-tune your approach and spot areas for improvement.

But hey, let's keep it real. Adaptation isn't always a walk in the park. It's about embracing the journey, bumps and all, with a mindset geared toward growth. Every challenge is a chance to learn, to tweak, and to come back stronger. So, when the going gets tough, remember: setbacks are just detours on the road to success. Keep pushing forward, and you'll get there, one step at a time!

5.6. Reflect and Learn

Now, let's talk about those roadblocks. Did you encounter any setbacks that made you want to throw in the towel? Take a moment to reflect on how you tackled those challenges. Did you muster up some resilience and find a way forward, or did you let them knock you down?

Here's the kicker: as you delve into this process, you might find yourself feeling a bit vulnerable. And guess what? That's totally okay! Embracing vulnerability is like flexing a muscle—it's uncomfortable at first, but it's essential for growth. So, don't shy away from acknowledging your mistakes or weaknesses. Instead, see them as stepping stones on your journey to becoming the best version of yourself.

And here's the secret sauce: adopt a growth mindset. Instead of viewing challenges as roadblocks, see them as opportunities for growth and learning. Every stumble is a chance to dust yourself off, learn something new, and come back stronger than before. So, roll up your sleeves, dive headfirst into reflection, and watch as you emerge wiser, stronger, and ready to take on whatever comes your way!.

5.7. Seek Feedback

Alright, let's dive into the feedback zone! Picture this: you're in the midst of a feedback conversation, and your radar is tuned to active listening mode. As you soak in the feedback, keep your ears perked for not just the words, but the vibe behind them. Remember, feedback isn't a finger-pointing game; it's like a treasure map leading you to valuable insights and perspectives.

Now, here's the scoop: don't be afraid to dig deeper. Ask those clarifying questions to make sure you're on the same page. Get those specifics, those juicy examples that paint the picture vividly. The more you understand, the better you can tweak your problem-solving prowess.

Once you've absorbed all that feedback goodness, take a breather. Reflect on it like you're pondering the mysteries of the universe. Think about how you can sprinkle some of that feedback magic into your problem-solving playbook. What tweaks can you make? What strategies can you finesse? It's all about turning those insights into action steps, baby!

And here's the kicker: each feedback loop is like a level-up potion in your career quest. By mastering the art of feedback, you're not just leveling up; you're unlocking a secret power-up that propels you to new heights. So, when you reach Chapter 7 of this book, you'll be strutting through your career journey like a boss, armed with feedback-fueled wisdom!

CHAPTER 4: Stay Motivated

Are you finding it increasingly difficult to muster up enthusiasm for your 9-to-5 grind? Trust me, you're not alone. The monotony of the same routine day in and day out can quickly take its toll, leaving even the most motivated individuals feeling drained and uninspired. Maybe you've started to resent your job, counting down the minutes until you can escape the office. Perhaps you find yourself going through the motions, feeling like a cog in the corporate machine. And let's not even get started on that overwhelming sense of exhaustion that seems to permeate every aspect of your life.

It's a slippery slope, isn't it? The more you hate your job, the more trapped you feel in it. The more trapped you feel, the more exhausted you become. And before you know it, you're caught in a downward spiral of negativity and despair. It's no wonder that feelings of depression can start to creep in, casting a shadow over even the brightest of days.

But fear not, my friend. Despite how bleak things may seem right now, there is hope on the horizon. In the next chapter, we're going to dive deep into some tried-and-true strategies for breaking free from the clutches of job-related despair and reclaiming your sense of purpose and fulfillment. From small changes you can implement in your daily routine to larger shifts in mindset and perspective, we'll explore a range of techniques designed to help you rediscover your passion for life.

So take heart, weary worker. You may feel like you're stuck in a never-ending cycle of misery right now, but brighter days are ahead. With a little guidance and a whole lot of determination, you can rise above the negativity and chart a course toward a brighter, more fulfilling future. So sit tight, grab a snack, and get ready to embark on a journey of self-discovery and transformation. The best is yet to come!.

3.1 Clarify Your Why

Ah, the age-old question—why work? It's not just about paying the bills, is it? No, it's about something deeper, something more meaningful. For many of us, it's about having the freedom to pursue our passions, to live life on our own terms. And what better way to achieve that than by building up our savings and investments? It's like laying the groundwork for our future selves, ensuring that we have the financial security to weather any storm and seize every opportunity that comes our way.

But wait, there's more! It's not just about squirreling away money for a rainy day. It's about creating passive income streams that keep the cash flowing, even when we're kicking back and enjoying life. Picture this: lounging on a sun-soaked beach, Mai Tai in hand, while your investments work their magic in the background. Now that's the dream, isn't it?

And speaking of dreams, what about those overseas travels? The thrill of exploring new cultures, sampling exotic cuisines, and soaking in breathtaking vistas—it's enough to make anyone's heart skip a beat. But here's the kicker: all those adventures require a bit of financial savvy. That's where our savings and investments come in handy, funding our globetrotting escapades and turning dreams into reality.

But hey, enough about me—what about you? What's your why? Maybe it's building your dream home, starting a family, or pursuing a passion project. Whatever it is, one thing's for sure: we're all in this journey called life together, and it's the dreams and aspirations that keep us pushing forward, striving for a brighter tomorrow. So here's to working smart, saving wisely, and living life to the fullest—cheers to us all!

3.2 Set Clear Goals

Alright, let's spice up the goal-setting game! Picture this: You're gearing up for a productive 9-to-6 grind, but before you dive in, let's talk goals. Clear goals are like the North Star—they keep you on track and fired up for success.

First things first, let's get SMART about it—specific, measurable, achievable, relevant, and time-bound. Break those big dreams into bite-sized chunks, making them easier to tackle and track. Trust me, it's like having your own personal roadmap to victory!

Now, grab a pen and paper (or your favorite app) and jot those goals down. Stick 'em where you can't miss 'em—on your desk, your fridge, or even as your screensaver. A little visual reminder never hurt anybody, right?

But hey, don't go it alone! Share your goals with a buddy, a work pal, or that wise mentor who always has your back. Having someone to cheer you on and keep you in check can make all the difference.

Next up, let's prioritize like a pro. Focus your energy on the tasks that move the needle the most. Break 'em down into baby steps and watch those milestones add up faster than you can say "goal-getter!"

And here's the secret sauce—flexibility. Life's a wild ride, so be ready to pivot and adjust those goals as needed. Stay nimble, stay adaptable, and keep your eyes on the prize.

Last but not least, let's paint a picture of success. Close your eyes and visualize crushing those goals like a boss. Feel the thrill of victory, the rush of accomplishment—it's all within reach, my friend.

So there you have it—goal-setting, spiced up and served with a side of motivation. With clear goals and a dash of determination, you're unstoppable in that 9-to-6 hustle!

3.4 Seek Growth Opportunities

Hey there, fellow growth-seeker! Ready to turn your 9-to-6 gig into a springboard for success? Buckle up, because we're diving headfirst into the exciting world of professional development.

First things first, let's talk about seizing those growth opportunities like a boss. It's all about raising your hand and shouting from the rooftops (or maybe just your cubicle) that you're hungry for more. Chat with your supervisor or swing by HR to chat about your career goals. Let 'em know you're eager to level up and ask about any juicy training programs or mentorship gigs they've got cooking.

But hey, don't stop there! Take the reins and seek out chances to flex those mental muscles outside of the usual training grind. Volunteer for new projects, scoop up extra responsibilities, or jump into cross-functional teams like a fearless explorer. Embrace the unknown, my friend, and watch those skills skyrocket!

Now, let's talk networking—aka your secret weapon for snagging those sweet growth gigs. Rub elbows with colleagues, mentors, and industry bigwigs who've got the inside scoop on all things career-boosting. Hit up industry events, cozy up to professional associations, and dive into online communities like a boss to expand your tribe and uncover new opportunities.

And here's a pro tip: never underestimate the power of feedback. Seek it out like it's going out of style, my friend! Whether it's from your boss, your peers, or that wise mentor who always tells it like it is, soak it up like a sponge and use it to fuel your growth journey.

Oh, and let's not forget about DIY learning! Dive into online courses, devour books and podcasts, and soak up knowledge like a boss. Master your craft, and who knows? Maybe you'll be ready to take that leap into a whole new adventure—one that's waiting for you in Chapter 7 of this book. So chin up, champ! The growth train is leaving the station, and you've got a front-row seat. Let's do this!

3.5 Celebrate Successes

Acknowledging your efforts not only boosts your confidence but also keeps that motivational fire burning bright.

But hey, why stop there? Spread the good vibes by sharing your achievements with others! Whether it's your work buddies, pals, or family, letting them in on your triumphs adds an extra layer of sweetness to the victory cake. And speaking of treats, don't forget to pamper yourself a bit. Treat yo'self to something special—a tasty meal, a little splurge, or maybe even a chill session doing something you love. Consider it a well-deserved reward for all your hard work.

Now, let's talk workplace vibes. Why not sprinkle some celebration magic around the office? Make it a thing to shout out and cheer on your colleagues' wins. Building a culture of celebration not only amps up the good vibes but also creates a supportive atmosphere where everyone feels valued and motivated to keep crushing it.

And remember, each success is a stepping stone in your journey of growth and progress. By embracing and celebrating your wins along the way, you're not just marking moments of achievement—you're crafting a narrative of personal and professional development. So go ahead, pop that imaginary champagne cork, and revel in the joy of your successes. Well, in Part 3, we'll delve deeper into how these celebrations tie into your bigger picture of financial freedom and living the life fullest. But hey, no spoilers—let's keep the excitement in check and focus on laying down some solid plans!

3.6 Stay Positive

Staying upbeat while clocking in those 9-to-6 hours can feel like a superpower sometimes, right? But fear not, my friend! Here are some nifty tips to keep that positivity train chugging along the tracks:

First up, let's talk gratitude. Take a moment each day to count your blessings, big and small. Whether it's the awesome squad of colleagues you've got or the fact that you can treat yourself to your favorite coffee, focusing on the good stuff can totally shift your vibe.

Now, when life throws those curveballs, let's hit 'em out of the park! Instead of seeing challenges as roadblocks, think of them as opportunities to flex those mental muscles. Embrace that growth mindset like a boss, and watch yourself conquer obstacles like a champ.

Oh, and speaking of champs, surround yourself with positive peeps who lift you higher. Whether it's your work buddies, mentors, or your ride-or-die crew, having that support system in place can turn even the toughest days into a walk in the park.

And hey, don't forget to show yourself some love too! Take time for self-care rituals that light you up inside, whether it's sweating it out at the gym, zoning out with your favorite tunes, or chilling with your fur babies. Taking care of numero uno is key to keeping that positivity tank topped up.

Last but not least, remember: focus on what you can control and let go of the rest. Instead of getting bogged down by stuff outside your sphere of influence, channel that energy into actions that move you forward. You've got this!

3.7 Find Support

Surrounding yourself with a fantastic network of colleagues, mentors, friends, and family members who truly get your professional journey can be like having a cheering squad, a guidance counselor, and a motivational speaker all rolled into one!

First up, let's talk about mentors and colleagues within your organization. These are the folks who've been there, done that, and got the T-shirt. They're invaluable sources of advice, wisdom, and support, ready to share their experiences and lend a helping hand when you're facing a tricky situation or need some direction.

And hey, don't stop there—venture out into the wider world of professional networks! Whether it's joining industry associations or hopping into online communities, these spaces are like treasure troves of knowledge and connections just waiting to be discovered. You'll meet like-minded souls, swap stories, and maybe even find your next career opportunity along the way.

But wait, there's more! Your friends and family aren't just there for Sunday barbecues and movie nights—they're also your rock when the going gets tough. Pour your heart out to them, share your wins and woes, and soak up all that love and support they're ready to dish out.

And speaking of camaraderie, don't underestimate the power of your fellow coworkers. Bonding over shared goals and experiences can create a sense of unity and solidarity that's downright magical. So why not organize a little get-together or start a support group? You'll be amazed at how much strength you can draw from each other.

And hey, if you hit a snag along the way, don't sweat it! We've got your back in the next chapter. Together, we'll tackle whatever challenges come your way and come out stronger on the other side. So keep that chin up, champ—you've got a whole squad of support behind you!

3.10 Visualize Success

Imagine this: you're sitting down, pen in hand, ready to sketch out the blueprint for your success. But where do you start? Simple—define what success means to you. Maybe it's scoring that dream job, getting recognized for your hard work, or making a positive impact on your team. Once you've got that vision locked in, it's time to add some color to the canvas.

Close your eyes and let your imagination run wild. Picture yourself living the dream. Is it lounging in luxury, cruising in a sports car, or savoring a five-star meal? Dive deep into the details. Feel the leather of the car seats, hear the clinking of glasses, taste the exquisite flavors dancing on your palate.

Now, let's kick it up a notch. Visualize the journey to success—the highs, the lows, and everything in between. See yourself conquering challenges like a boss, overcoming obstacles with grit and grace. Feel the rush of accomplishment, the swell of pride, the warmth of fulfillment—it's all within reach.

But hold up, we're not done yet. Break down your vision into bite-sized pieces. See yourself tackling each step with confidence, charting your course with precision. And when roadblocks pop up (because let's face it, they always do), visualize yourself plowing through them like a champ, unfazed and unstoppable.

Here's the kicker—make visualization a daily habit. Set aside time to paint your success story, morning, noon, or night. The more you see it, feel it, believe it, the closer you'll get to living it. So grab your mental paintbrush and let's turn that vision into reality, one vivid stroke at a time.

CHAPTER 5: Handle Depression

Alright, buckle up because we're diving into one of the juiciest topics around—especially for the younger crowd. In a world where everything moves at the speed of light, it's no surprise that folks want it all, and they want it now. I mean, who doesn't dream of striking it rich with minimal effort, right? But here's the reality check: life doesn't come with a fast-forward button. That's why in our previous chat, I stressed the importance of setting realistic goals.

Let's get real for a sec. Burnout is no joke. When you're hustling non-stop, juggling work, family, and relationships, it's easy to feel like you're drowning. And trust me, that's a dark place nobody wants to go. It's like falling into a deep hole, and if you don't pull yourself out, things can get downright dangerous.

So, let's look out for each other, okay? Let's talk about the tough stuff, break down those barriers, and remind each other that it's okay to slow down and take a breather. Because at the end of the day, nothing—not even that elusive pot of gold—is worth sacrificing our mental and emotional well-being for. So let's keep the conversation going, support one another, and remember that we're all in this crazy ride called life together.

5.1 Seek Professional Help

Hey there! So, you're thinking about reaching out for some support in dealing with depression? That's a fantastic first step! Let's break it down in a friendly and easy-to-digest way.

First off, let's find you the right mental health pro. Look for someone who's a pro at treating depression and knows their way around busy schedules. Ask around or hit up the internet to find therapists who specialize in balancing work demands with mental health care.

Once you've got some names, it's time to reach out! Shoot them a message or give them a call to see if they're available and if they're a good fit for you.

Now, scheduling can be a bit tricky with your 9-to-5 gig, right? No worries! Look for therapists who offer flexible hours like early mornings, evenings, or even weekends. And hey, don't forget about teletherapy—it's like therapy but with the comfy convenience of your own space!

Before your first session, jot down any questions or concerns you want to chat about. And when you meet your therapist, be real with them about what you're going through. They're here to help, so spill the beans!

Together, you'll come up with a game plan tailored just for you. Think techniques like cognitive-behavioral therapy (CBT), mindfulness, or maybe even exploring medication options.

Now, here's the kicker—consistency is key! Show up to your sessions like clockwork and put in the work between sessions. You've got this! And remember, seeking help is a brave move, and your therapist's got your back every step of the way. You're not alone in this journey!

5.2 Establish a Routine

Navigating through the twists and turns of depression can feel like walking a tightrope, but hey, consistency can be your safety net. Start your day on the right foot with a morning routine that's all about setting the vibe. Whether it's greeting the sunrise at the crack of dawn, cozying up with some meditation or journaling, or whipping up a breakfast that screams "I got this," find what works for you and stick with it.

Now, onto the daily grind. Work doesn't have to be a never-ending marathon. Break it down into bite-sized pieces, sprinkle in some breaks, and voilà—suddenly, it feels a lot more manageable. Take a breather, stretch those limbs, or sneak in a stroll outside. Trust me, your brain will thank you for it.

But life's not all about work, right? It's about finding those moments of bliss in between. Dive into activities that light up your soul—whether it's sweating it out at the gym, geeking out over your favorite hobbies, or simply soaking up the good vibes with your squad. And hey, don't forget about sleep! A solid bedtime routine can work wonders for your mental well-being. Wind down with a good book or some chill tunes to signal to your body that it's time to catch those Z's.

Now, here's the kicker—flexibility. Some days, sticking to your routine might feel as easy as pie. Other days, not so much. And that's okay! Cut yourself some slack, roll with the punches, and adjust as needed. After all, life's all about finding your rhythm, dancing to your own beat, and knowing when to shake things up a bit. You got this!

5.3 Prioritize Self-Care

Let's talk about treating yourself like the VIP you are! One awesome way to do this is by sprinkling some self-care into your daily routine. Picture this: carving out a little slice of time each day to do something that makes your heart happy. Whether it's diving into a good book, taking a leisurely stroll, striking a yoga pose, or jamming out to your favorite tunes, make it a non-negotiable part of your day. Trust me, your mental and emotional well-being will thank you for it!

Now, let's get physical! Did you know that moving your body is like giving your brain a big ol' hug? It's true! Regular exercise has superhero powers when it comes to kicking anxiety and depression to the curb. So, why not sneak in some movement whenever you can? Whether it's a lunchtime walk, a quick workout sesh before or after work, or busting a move in a weekend fitness class, find what gets your heart pumping and roll with it.

And hey, let's not forget about the fuel that powers your amazingness—food! Loading up on nutritious goodies like fruits, veggies, whole grains, and lean proteins not only keeps your body happy but also puts a smile on your face. Say "see ya later" to processed junk and hello to foods that'll have you feeling like a million bucks.

Last but definitely not least, let's cozy up with some Zzz's. Beauty sleep isn't just a saying—it's science! Creating a bedtime ritual and crafting the perfect sleep setup can work wonders for your mind and body. Think unplugging from screens, unwinding with some deep breaths or meditation, and snuggling up in a cool, dark, and quiet sleep sanctuary.

5.4 Practice Mindfulness

Hey there, friend! Life can sometimes feel like a wild rollercoaster, especially when those heavy thoughts of despair and uncertainty start crashing in. But fear not! Enter mindfulness—a superhero technique that can swoop in and lighten the load of depression.

Picture this: you're knee-deep in the workday chaos, but you carve out a little oasis of calm. Find your zen zone, even if it's just a tiny corner of your office. Close those peepers and dive into a mini-meditation. Inhale, exhale—let those breaths be your anchor. Allow thoughts to stroll in and out without judgment, gently steering your focus back to the breath. It's like a mini-vacation for your mind, soothing the storm of depression with a sprinkle of serenity.

Now, here's another trick up our mindfulness sleeve—conscious awareness. As you tackle your to-dos, be the superhero of the present moment. Whether you're crafting emails, diving into meetings, or sipping that life-saving coffee, be all in. Break free from the worry loop, and embrace each moment with clarity and focus. It's like a mental superhero cape, helping you navigate the challenges of depression with style.

But hold up, we're not done yet! Mindfulness isn't just for the office—it's an everyday superstar. Dive into the joy of lunchtime flavors, savoring each bite like a foodie on a mission. Sneak in a nature break during your workday hustle, immersing yourself in the sights and sounds around you. These mindful moments become your secret weapons, bringing peace and tranquility to the chaos.

And here's the golden rule—be kind to yourself. We all stumble sometimes, and that's okay. Embrace mindfulness as your gentle sidekick on this journey. With a dash of compassion and a sprinkle of patience, you'll be navigating the twists and turns of depression like a true mindfulness superhero!

5.5 Stay Active

Ever thought about ditching the elevator and taking the stairs? Or maybe swapping your coffee break for a quick stroll around the block? These mini bursts of movement might seem small, but trust me, they add up!

Now, let's get real about exercise—it's gotta be fun, right? Ever tried your hand at yoga, or maybe busted a move on the dance floor? Finding workouts that you actually enjoy makes sticking to them a whole lot easier. So why not explore different activities until you find your fitness soulmate?

But hey, we're all human here. Ever felt a twinge of guilt when you missed a workout? It happens! That's why it's crucial to set realistic goals and give yourself a big ol' pat on the back for every little victory. You're doing great, buddy!

Oh, and here's a game-changer: enlist a workout buddy! Whether it's a pal, a fam member, or even a coworker, having someone by your side can turn exercise into a party. They'll keep you accountable, cheer you on, and make those sweat sessions way more fun.

And guess what? Staying active doesn't always mean hitting the gym. Sometimes, it's as simple as getting your hands dirty in the garden or chasing your furball around the living room. Every little bit counts!

So there you have it, friend—staying active doesn't have to be a chore. With a sprinkle of creativity, a dash of self-compassion, and a pinch of support, you'll be living your healthiest, happiest life in no time.

5.6 Consider Medication

When you're pondering the medication route, it's like standing at a crossroads, isn't it? You're asking yourself all sorts of questions—Is this the right path for me? Are there other trails I should explore first? These doubts are as common as morning coffee cravings, and it's A-OK to take your time mulling them over.

Now, here's where the cavalry rides in: your healthcare squad. Yep, your doctor or psychiatrist is like your trusty sidekick, ready to lend an ear and offer sage advice. They'll help you navigate the maze of medication options, shed light on potential perks and pitfalls, and tailor a plan that's as unique as you are.

And hey, let's get one thing straight: deciding to give medication a shot doesn't mean you're waving the white flag of surrender. Au contraire! It's a brave move—a sign that you're taking charge of your mental well-being and saying, "Hey, I deserve to feel better." And if you find yourself riding an emotional rollercoaster along the way—complete with loops of relief, drops of anxiety, and twists of uncertainty—know that it's all part of the ride in life.

PART 2 KEEP IT GOING

CHAPTER 6: Make it adventurous

Let's face it, the daily grind of a 9-to-6 job can sometimes feel like a one-way ticket to Snoozeville. But hey, who says we have to settle for a snooze fest? Injecting a little adventure into our lives might just be the secret sauce to surviving those less-than-exciting gigs. We get it—we've been there, done that, and got the coffee stain on the T-shirt to prove it. The routine of commuting, doing the same tasks, and punching the clock can zap the zest right out of us.

But fear not, fellow adventurers! Switching up our routines isn't just about shaking off the cobwebs—it's about reclaiming our mojo, finding that balance, and unleashing our inner rockstars. Because let's be real, in today's world where change is the only constant, sticking to the same-old, same-old just won't cut it anymore.

So why change things up? Well, for starters, it's like hitting the refresh button on life. It's about staying nimble, staying sharp, and staying sane in a world that's spinning faster than a Beyoncé dance routine. By embracing change, we're not just surviving—we're thriving. We're opening ourselves up to new possibilities, new experiences, and new horizons.

And let's not forget the thrill of it all! Changing things up adds a dash of spice to our daily dish of existence. It's like swapping out that bland sandwich for a gourmet meal—it's exciting, it's invigorating, and it's oh-so-delicious. Whether it's shaking up our work routine, picking up a new hobby, or taking the scenic route to the office, these little changes can make a world of difference.

6.1 Assess current routine

Let's talk about routines, shall we? You know, those mundane day-to-day habits that can sometimes suck the life out of you faster than a vacuum cleaner on turbo mode. But fear not! We're here to shake things up and inject a little zest back into your routine.

First up, let's take a gander at your daily grind. Is your commute a snooze-fest of the same ol' scenery? Do you find yourself stuck in a lunchtime rut, hitting up the same old joint day in and day out? And after work, is your plan as predictable as the plot of a Hallmark movie marathon?

Well, my friend, it's time to break free from the monotony! Spice things up like you're adding cayenne pepper to your morning coffee. Take a different route to work, explore a new lunch spot, or shake up your post-work plans. Ever thought about hitting the gym on a whim, or maybe trying out that quirky yoga class you've been eyeing? The world is your oyster, and it's high time you started cracking it open!

So, next time you find yourself stuck in the same old routine, remember: variety is the spice of life. Embrace the unexpected, sprinkle in a dash of adventure, and watch as your days transform from dull to dynamite!.

6.2 Recommend to change routine every 3 month

Imagine feeling stuck in a repetitive cycle, where each day feels like a carbon copy of the last. It's easy to become demotivated and uninspired when faced with the same tasks and environments day in and day out. By changing routines every three months, employees inject freshness and excitement into their work lives.

At first glance, the idea of shaking up your routine might seem a bit daunting, right? I mean, who doesn't love their cozy little comfort zone? But here's the thing: change can be seriously invigorating! Once you take that leap, you'll find yourself diving headfirst into a whirlwind of new experiences and challenges. Each turn of the wheel opens doors to fresh perspectives, hones your time management skills, and helps you figure out what really gets your motor running.

But wait, there's more! This whole routine-switcheroo thing isn't just about jumping blindly into the unknown. Nope, it's about taking a step back every now and then to reflect on how far you've come. It's like a journey of self-discovery, where you figure out what environments and methods work best for you. Talk about a recipe for resilience and adaptability, two things you definitely need to conquer the 9-to-6 grind.

And here's the kicker: by mixing up your routine every three months, you're not just along for the ride—you're driving the dang bus! You get to call the shots, shaping your work life to fit your evolving needs and dreams. That sense of control? It's like rocket fuel for your sense of fulfillment and satisfaction.

So yeah, changing things up every few months might seem a bit out there, but trust me—it's the secret sauce to beating the blahs of routine and burnout. It's your ticket to embracing change, building resilience, and finding your own little slice of work-life harmony. So why wait? Let's shake things up and make some magic happen!

CHAPTER 7: Job hopping

You've been grinding away at your job for a solid two years, and now you're feeling that itch for something new, something exciting. Enter job hopping—your ticket to shaking things up and getting a fresh perspective on your career journey. Sure, it's not always the easiest decision, and some folks might raise an eyebrow or two, but trust me, there's a method to this madness.

Let's dive into why job hopping isn't just about restlessness or commitment issues—it's about unlocking a world of opportunities. Imagine feeling like you're stuck in Groundhog Day, where every workday blends into the next with no end in sight. Sound familiar? Well, by hopping from one job to another, you're breaking free from that cycle of monotony. Each new role brings with it a fresh set of challenges, a different office vibe, and a chance to rediscover your mojo.

But wait, there's more! Job hopping isn't just about escaping the mundane—it's also a sneaky way to level up your skills. In a traditional 9-to-6 gig, you might find yourself stuck in a rut, doing the same old tasks day in and day out. Boring, right? Well, by jumping ship and exploring new opportunities, you're exposing yourself to a smorgasbord of learning experiences. New industries, new technologies, new ways of doing things—the possibilities are endless. And hey, who doesn't love adding a few shiny new skills to their resume?

Now, let's talk money. We all know that feeling when you've been busting your butt at the same job for ages, and yet your paycheck seems to be stuck in neutral. Frustrating, isn't it? Well, guess what? Job hopping can be your secret weapon for snagging that sweet, sweet raise. By putting yourself out there and exploring new job prospects, you're opening yourself up to better pay, juicier benefits, and maybe even a corner office with a view. Cha-ching!

So, there you have it—job hopping isn't just a flight of fancy; it's a strategic move to keep your career fresh, your skills sharp, and your bank account happy. So go ahead, take that leap of faith, and see where the adventure takes you. Who knows? Your next job hop might just be the best decision you ever make!

7.1 Increase Salary

So, you're eyeing that shiny new job, right? Well, here's the scoop: aim high when it comes to negotiating that salary. Shoot for the stars and aim for at least a 30% bump (or more if you can swing it). Think about it like this—consider your living costs, factor in pesky things like inflation, and crunch the numbers to figure out just how much moolah you can stash away each month.

Now, here's where the magic happens: once you've snagged that sweet salary boost, don't go on a spending spree worthy of a Hollywood blockbuster. Nope, instead, stick to your guns and maintain those sensible spending habits. Then, kick it up a notch by turbocharging your savings rate. Why, you ask? Because we're not in the game to work 'til we drop—we're here to live it up and retire like royalty, with a fat stack of passive income cushioning our golden years.

So, in the grand scheme of things, it's all about setting yourself up for success. Negotiate like a pro, save like a champ, and dream big about that early retirement filled with lazy days and endless adventures. Because hey, life's too short to spend it all stuck behind a desk, am I right? Go get 'em, tiger!

7.2 Explore Different Industries

Ah, the age-old dilemma: feeling like you're stuck in a job rut, despite bouncing around different companies and approaches. Ever felt that way? It's like trying on different shoes but still feeling like something's not quite right. Sure, you could venture into different industries, but let's be real—it's like diving into a whole new world. It takes effort, energy, and a whole lot of grit to get up to speed.

And let's face it—we're not exactly getting any younger here. Time's ticking, and ain't nobody got time for unnecessary stress, am I right? So before you go jumping ship, think long and hard about whether it's worth the hassle. But hey, if you're feeling jazzed and pumped about the idea, why not give it a whirl? Life's too short for what-ifs!

But here's the golden rule: never settle for less than what you're worth. If you're gonna take the plunge into uncharted waters, make sure the paycheck matches the risk. After all, ain't nobody got time to be broke! So go ahead, embrace the adventure, but always keep your wallet in check. Who said adulting had to be boring, huh?

7.3 Test Company Culture

Alright, so you've landed yourself a shiny new job, huh? That's awesome! It's like dipping your toes into a new adventure. But hold your horses—before you go all in, let's talk probation periods. You know, that little trial phase most jobs have before they seal the deal and make you a permanent fixture.

During this trial run, take a good look around. Consider the nitty-gritty details like how much time you're spending on that daily commute. Is it a hop, skip, and a jump away, or are you embarking on a cross-country expedition every morning? And speaking of costs, let's not forget about the ol' wallet. Take a peek at the cost of living in your new digs. Are you gonna need to tighten those purse strings a bit, or are you golden?

But wait, there's more! Don't overlook those sneaky hidden costs. You know, the ones that lurk in the shadows like parking fees that could rival a small mortgage payment or that swanky gym membership you just had to have. It's all about considering the full picture before you say "I do" to that full-time gig. So take your time, weigh your options, and make sure this new job is the perfect fit for you.

7.4 Adaptability

stepping into a new gig can feel like grooving to a fresh beat, right? But hey, nobody mastered the tango overnight! Take a chill pill, go with the flow, and let yourself settle into the rhythm. Remember those pearls of wisdom I dropped in the first part of this book? Those babies are like your loyal sidekick on this journey. Brush 'em off, give 'em a spin, and watch as they sprinkle a little magic on your path forward.

Mastering adaptability means staying open to new experiences and growth opportunities. It's about tackling each task, each project, with a flexible mindset, ready to pivot and evolve as needed. Maybe it means picking up some new skills, adapting to different team vibes, or even setting some fresh boundaries to keep your sanity intact.

And hey, having a solid support squad can be a game-changer in staying adaptable. Whether it's colleagues or mentors who've been around the job block, having folks who get it can be a total lifesaver. They'll dish out advice, share war stories, and be your go-to sounding board when things get a little rocky. So, grab your dancing shoes, embrace the changes, and get ready to rock this new gig!

However, it's also essential to acknowledge the emotional toll that constant adaptation can take. Job hopping can sometimes lead to feelings of restlessness, imposter syndrome, or even burnout. It's okay to seek support, whether through therapy, self-care practices, or simply confiding in trusted friends or family members.

CHAPTER 8: Financial Freedom

Imagine the feeling of excitement and anticipation that comes with envisioning a future where you have achieved financial security and freedom. Picture yourself being able to afford the things you've always dreamed of, whether it's buying a house, traveling the world, or supporting your loved ones. This vision acts as a beacon, guiding your actions and decisions in the present.

When you have clear financial goals in mind, each day at work takes on a new significance. Rather than simply going through the motions, you see each task as a stepping stone towards your ultimate objectives. Whether it's meeting deadlines, taking on extra projects, or seeking out opportunities for growth and advancement, every action becomes infused with purpose and meaning. You understand that the sacrifices and effort you put in now are investments in your future financial well-being.

Moreover, having long-term financial goals can help you weather the inevitable challenges and setbacks that come with any job. When faced with difficulties or moments of doubt, you can draw strength from your vision of the future. Remind yourself of why you started on this journey in the first place and the rewards that await you at the end of the road. This perspective shift can be incredibly empowering, allowing you to persevere through tough times with resilience and determination.

Additionally, setting financial goals can foster a sense of control and autonomy in your life. Rather than feeling like a passive bystander in your career, you become the architect of your own destiny. You have a clear roadmap for where you want to go and the steps you need to take to get there. This sense of agency can be incredibly empowering, boosting your confidence and morale as you navigate the ups and downs of your job.

8.1 Budgeting

When individuals set clear financial goals, such as saving for a vacation, buying a home, or building an emergency fund, it gives them something tangible to work towards beyond the daily grind of their job.

Moreover, budgeting allows individuals to take control of their finances and make intentional decisions about how they allocate their resources. This sense of control can be empowering, especially in a job where they may feel limited or constrained. By creating a budget, individuals can track their income and expenses, identify areas where they can cut back or save more, and ultimately, make progress towards their financial goals.

In the context of a 9-6 job, where the routine can sometimes feel overwhelming or draining, having financial goals provides a sense of motivation and purpose. It gives individuals something to look forward to outside of work, whether it's saving up for a dream vacation or working towards financial independence. This can help alleviate some of the stress or monotony associated with the daily grind and provide a sense of fulfillment and accomplishment.

Additionally, budgeting can also serve as a form of self-care in the context of a demanding job. By taking the time to manage their finances and plan for the future, individuals are investing in their well-being and long-term happiness. It allows them to prioritize their needs and goals, whether it's setting aside money for personal development, leisure activities, or retirement.

8.2 Investments

Picture this: you're sitting at your desk, scrolling through spreadsheets or answering emails, and while you may be focused on the task at hand, there's a part of you that yearns for something more, something beyond the confines of your office walls. That's where investments come in. By setting clear financial goals, such as saving for retirement, building an emergency fund, or investing in assets like stocks or real estate, you're not just working for a paycheck; you're working towards a future where your money works for you.

Imagine the excitement of watching your investment portfolio grow over time, knowing that every dollar you put in is a step closer to your financial dreams. It adds a layer of meaning to your daily efforts, knowing that you're not just trading time for money, but actively building wealth that can support you and your loved ones for years to come.

Of course, investing also comes with its fair share of challenges and uncertainties. There may be moments of doubt or anxiety, especially during market downturns or when faced with complex investment decisions. Yet, it's precisely in these moments that the discipline and resilience cultivated through your 9-6 job can serve you well. Just as you tackle challenges at work with determination and adaptability, so too can you navigate the ups and downs of the investment world with patience and sound judgment.

Moreover, investing can offer a sense of autonomy and control that may feel lacking in a traditional corporate setting. While your job may come with its own set of rules and hierarchies, your investment portfolio is yours to shape and manage as you see fit. Whether you prefer a hands-on approach, actively researching and selecting individual investments, or a more passive strategy, entrusting your money to index funds or robo-advisors, the choice is yours.

In essence, integrating investments as financial goals into your life alongside a 9-6 job is about more than just securing your financial future; it's about infusing your daily grind with purpose and direction. It's about recognizing that your time and effort are valuable resources, not just for today, but for the tomorrows yet to come.

8.3 Reduce debt

Firstly, it's crucial to face the reality of your financial situation. Acknowledge any outstanding debts, whether they're from credit cards, loans, or other sources. This initial assessment might stir up feelings of anxiety or frustration, but it's the first step toward regaining control.

Next, set clear and achievable financial goals. Break down your debt into manageable chunks and establish a timeline for paying it off. Visualizing your progress can provide motivation and a sense of accomplishment along the way. Moreover, prioritize your debts based on interest rates or other factors to strategize repayment effectively. This proactive approach can instill a sense of empowerment and control over your financial future.

While working a 9-6 job, finding additional sources of income or cutting expenses can accelerate debt repayment. This might mean taking on a side hustle, freelancing, or selling unused belongings. Adjusting spending habits can be challenging, especially if it involves sacrificing luxuries or conveniences. However, focusing on the long-term benefits of financial freedom can help alleviate any short-term discomfort.

Building a support system can also be invaluable during this journey. Surround yourself with friends, family, or online communities who understand your financial goals and can offer encouragement and advice. Sharing your progress and setbacks with others can provide accountability and motivation to stay on track, especially during difficult moments.

Lastly, celebrate small victories along the way. Whether it's paying off a credit card or reaching a savings milestone, acknowledging your progress reinforces positive financial habits and boosts morale

8.4 Emergency fund

Midst the hustle and bustle, unexpected expenses or emergencies can arise, causing stress and uncertainty. Having an emergency fund acts as a financial cushion, offering reassurance during challenging times.

Imagine the relief one might feel knowing they have a financial buffer to rely on if faced with unexpected medical bills, car repairs, or sudden job loss. It's like having a safety net beneath a tightrope walker; even if they stumble, they have something to catch them before they fall too far. This sense of security allows individuals to focus on their job without constant worry about what might happen if the unexpected occurs.

Building an emergency fund requires discipline and commitment, much like sticking to a demanding work schedule. It involves setting aside a portion of each paycheck, sometimes sacrificing immediate wants for future security. While it may seem daunting at first, the sense of accomplishment and peace of mind that comes with watching the fund grow can be incredibly empowering.

Imagine the sense of pride and relief as the emergency fund reaches its target amount, knowing that you've taken a proactive step towards financial stability. It's like reaching the peak of a mountain after a challenging climb; the view from the top is breathtaking, and the journey, though arduous, was undoubtedly worth it. This fund not only provides financial security but also serves as a reminder of one's ability to set goals and achieve them, bolstering confidence both inside and outside the workplace.

In the unpredictable landscape of modern life, having an emergency fund is like having a flashlight in the dark – it illuminates the path forward, offering clarity and security in times of uncertainty.

You've been grinding away, day after day, pouring your heart and soul into your 9-to-5 job. It's been a whirlwind of deadlines, meetings, and endless to-do lists, with each day blending into the next. But amidst the chaos, you've been absorbing every experience, every challenge, and every triumph, carving out a path for yourself in the corporate jungle.

Now, though, it's time to press pause on the hustle and bustle of everyday life and embrace the simple joy of living. And here's the thing—you don't need a fat bank account to do it. Life is an adventure waiting to be explored, filled with moments of laughter, excitement, and wonder, just waiting for you to seize them.

Sure, you might not have months of vacation time stashed away, but that doesn't mean you can't make the most of the time you do have. Take a cue from the wise and plan ahead, strategically using your precious PTO to escape the daily grind. And when you do, don't be afraid to treat yourself to a stay at a luxurious hotel. It's a chance to pamper yourself, to revel in the lap of luxury, and to recharge your batteries for the road ahead.

But here's the thing: while indulging yourself is all well and good, it's important to stay mindful of your budget. It's easy to get caught up in the allure of luxury and overspend in the heat of the moment. So, before you book that penthouse suite or splurge on a fancy dinner, take a moment to check in with your finances. Make sure you're not stretching yourself too thin and that every indulgence remains within your means.

And let's not forget the therapeutic release that comes from commiserating with your fellow office warriors about those less-than-ideal bosses. It's a chance to bond over shared experiences, to find humor in the absurdities of corporate life, and to remind yourself that you're not alone in the struggle.

So, as you embark on this journey of self-indulgence and adventure, remember this: life is what you make of it. It's about finding joy in the small moments, embracing the adventures that await, and always staying true to yourself—even when faced with those frustrating bosses. After all, you've earned it.

In the hustle and bustle of the daily grind, employees often find themselves caught up in a whirlwind of tasks, deadlines, and responsibilities. This continuous cycle can lead to burnout and decreased productivity over time.

During holiday breaks, employees have the chance to step away from the demands of their job and focus on themselves. Whether it's spending quality time with loved ones, pursuing hobbies and interests, or simply relaxing and unwinding, these breaks offer a valuable respite from the stresses of work life. This time away allows individuals to recharge their batteries both physically and mentally, enabling them to return to work with renewed energy and enthusiasm.

Moreover, holiday breaks provide employees with the opportunity to gain perspective and reflect on their professional goals and aspirations. Taking a step back from the daily routine allows individuals to reassess their priorities, evaluate their career trajectory, and consider any necessary adjustments or changes they may want to make. This introspective process can lead to increased job satisfaction and a greater sense of fulfillment in the long run.

Additionally, holiday breaks foster a healthy work-life balance, which is essential for overall well-being and job satisfaction. By dedicating time to activities outside of work, such as travel, leisure, and personal development, employees can cultivate a sense of fulfillment and fulfillment in their lives outside of the office. This balance not only promotes happiness and mental health but also contributes to increased productivity and job performance when employees return to work.

CHAPTER 10: Branded Clothes

Clothes, often underestimated, can play a significant role in shaping one's daily experience. Investing in high-quality clothing isn't just about aesthetics; it's about cultivating a mindset of self-care and empowerment that can positively influence how you feel throughout the day.

Picture this: You wake up early in the morning, facing another busy day at work. As you open your closet, instead of rummaging through a pile of worn-out garments, your eyes fall on a carefully curated selection of high-quality pieces. Each item is not just a piece of fabric, but a reflection of your personal style and attention to detail. The texture is soft, the seams are sturdy, and the fit is just right. As you slip into these clothes, you feel a sense of confidence wash over you, setting the tone for the day ahead.

Throughout the day, the comfort and durability of your clothing become apparent. You move with ease, whether you're rushing to meetings or sitting at your desk for hours on end. Unlike cheaper alternatives that may wear out quickly or lose their shape, these garments maintain their integrity, allowing you to focus on your tasks without distractions. Moreover, knowing that you've invested in quality gives you a sense of pride, reminding you that you deserve the best in every aspect of your life, including your wardrobe.

But it's not just about practicality; there's a psychological aspect to wearing high-quality clothes as well. The attention to detail and craftsmanship behind each piece can serve as a daily reminder of your worth and value. In a world where the line between work and personal life often blurs, these clothes become a form of self-expression, a way to reclaim your identity amidst the demands of the corporate world. They allow you to assert your individuality and creativity, even in a professional setting, fostering a sense of fulfillment and satisfaction.

Ultimately, buying high-quality clothes isn't just a transaction; it's an investment in yourself and your well-being. It's a statement that you prioritize comfort, confidence, and self-respect in every aspect of your life, including your daily attire.

CHAPTER 11: Invest in gadgets

Amidst the allure of the latest gadgets, there's a voice of reason—a reminder that you don't always need the shiniest, newest toy to find enjoyment and utility. Sure, the latest iPhone or Apple Watch may boast dazzling features and sleek design, but here's a secret: you can often achieve similar satisfaction with a brand-new older model.

Think about it. By opting for a slightly older model that still supports the latest updates, you're not just saving a pretty penny; you're investing in a debt-free future. You're channeling those savings into your life savings, inching closer to financial freedom with each mindful purchase.

In a world where consumerism often reigns supreme, this approach is a breath of fresh air. It's about prioritizing long-term stability over short-term gratification, about finding joy not in the fleeting rush of novelty, but in the steady progress towards your goals.

So, as you navigate the ever-changing landscape of tech, remember this: you don't need the latest and greatest to feel the joy of discovery. Sometimes, all it takes is a brand-new older model, a nod to the past with an eye towards the future. And in that simple choice lies the power to sustain not just a 9-to-5 job, but a debt-free, fulfilling life.

CHAPTER 12: Cash Cow

Indeed, the gadget you've just acquired isn't just a personal indulgence—it's a tool for success in the digital sphere. With its cutting-edge features and capabilities, it becomes the linchpin of your content creation strategy. Whether it's high-quality photos, engaging videos, or insightful reviews, your new gadget empowers you to produce top-notch content that resonates with your audience.

Think about it: crisp images that capture the essence of the latest tech trends, immersive videos that showcase the functionalities of your recommended gadgets, and detailed reviews that guide your followers in their purchasing decisions. With your newfound tool in hand, you're not just keeping up with the competition—you're setting the standard for quality content creation.

And as your content gains traction on social media, so too does your influence and credibility. Your followers look to you as a trusted source of tech wisdom, eagerly awaiting your recommendations and insights. It's a symbiotic relationship—the more value you provide, the more your following grows, and the more opportunities arise for monetization through affiliate marketing, sponsored content, or direct sales.

So, while acquiring the latest gadget may seem like a splurge at first glance, it's actually an investment in your digital presence and future success. With it, you're equipped to produce content that captivates, educates, and inspires—a content creator poised for growth and prosperity in the ever-evolving landscape of social media.

CHAPTER 13: Wrap Up

As we wrap up the final chapter of this book, let's reflect on some nuggets of wisdom that can add a little sparkle to your journey ahead. Life can throw some curveballs, right? But hey, even if you weren't born with a silver spoon, you've got what it takes to navigate those twists and turns. Sometimes, you gotta put on your game face, tackle that desk job, and show it who's boss!

Now, let's talk about the green stuff—money, honey! If you've got a little extra cash lying around, why not put it to work? Investing wisely could mean waving hello to a retirement filled with cozy passive income streams. Cha-ching!

But wait, hold the phone! In the hustle and bustle, don't forget to take care of numero uno—you! Your health is your wealth, so make sure to sprinkle in some self-love along the way. Remember, you've only got one shot at this thing called life. It's okay if you miss out on a few things, but keep your eyes peeled for those golden opportunities. Plan for them, chase after them, and make 'em count!

And last but not least, let's talk possibilities. Spoiler alert: they're endless! Sure, there might be a bump or two in the road, but with a dollop of determination and a pinch of positivity, you'll find that anything is possible. So buckle up, champ! Life's one wild ride, and you're the one driving. Here's to embracing the adventure, making memories, and writing your own epic tale—one chapter at a time. Cheers to you!

About the Author

Step into the world of personal growth and empowerment alongside Armie Bright, a dynamic voice in the realm of self-help literature. With his relatable anecdotes and practical tips, Armie Bright doesn't just tell you how to succeed—he takes you by the hand and guides you on a journey of self-discovery and transformation. Get ready to laugh, learn, and leap forward as you explore Armie Bright's empowering insights. Join the adventure today and start hustle the life you've always wanted!